1,000 L

W9-BSC-684

DISCARD

31.32

UNCOVERING THE PAST:
ANALYZING PRIMARY SOURCES

IMMIGRATION

LIZANN FLATT

Crabtree Publishing Company

www.crabtreebooks.com

Author: Lizann Flatt
**Publishing plan research and
    development:** Reagan Miller
Editor-in-Chief: Lionel Bender
Editors: Simon Adams, Anastasia Suen
Proofreaders: Laura Booth,
    Wendy Scavuzzo
Project coordinator: Kelly Spence
Design and photo research: Ben White
Production: Kim Richardson
**Production coordinator and
    prepress technician:** Ken Wright
Print coordinator: Margaret Amy Salter

Consultant: Amie Wright,
The New York Public Library

This book was produced for
Crabtree Publishing Company by
Bender Richardson White

Photographs and reproductions:
Front Cover: Wikimedia Commons (Hettie Dreyer)
Interior: Dreamstime.com: 12 middle left (Typhoonski); 20 middle right (Linda Morland). Getty Images: 40 middle rtight (John Moore). Library of Congress: 1 middle (LC-USZ62-11203); 3 bottom middle (LC-DIG-highsm-14242); 4, 6 top left (pnp-ggbain.03252); 8, 10, 12 top left (pnp-ppmsca.17886); 14, 16 top left (LC-USZC4-9866); 18, 20, 22 top left (LC-USZ62-11203); 23 top (pnp-ppmsca.17886); 24, 26, 28, 30 top left (LC-USZ62-11203); 30 bottom left (LC-USZC4-9866); 32, 34 top left (LC-USZC2-1066); 35 bottom (LC-DIG-nclc-04133); 36 top left (LC-USZC2-1066). Shutterstock.com: 1 full page (Petrov Stanislav); 38, 40 top left (Julien_N). Topfoto: 4–5 (TopFoto); 6 bottom right (The Image Works); 7 bottom (World History Archive); 8–9, 10 middle right, 11 bottom (The Granger Collection); 13 bottom (The Image Works); 14–15 middle, 16 top right, 17 bottom, 18–19, 21 bottom (The Granger Collection); 22 bottom (Topham Picturepoint); 24 middle, 25 bottom, 26 middle, (The Granger Collection); 27 bottom (Topfoto); 28 bottom right, 29 bottom (The Granger Collection); 31 bottom (HIP); 32–33, 34 middle right (The Granger Collection); 36 middle left (The Image Works); 37 bottom (United Archives); 38–39, 41 bottom (The Image Works).
Graphics: Stefan Chabluk

Library and Archives Canada Cataloguing in Publication

Flatt, Lizann, author
    Immigration / Lizann Flatt.

(Uncovering the past: analyzing primary sources)
Includes index.
Issued in print and electronic formats.
ISBN 978-0-7787-1550-4 (bound).--ISBN 978-0-7787-1554-2 (pbk.).--
ISBN 978-1-4271-1602-4 (pdf).--ISBN 978-1-4271-1598-0 (html)

        1. United States--Emigration and immigration--History--19th
century--Juvenile literature. 2. Canada--Emigration and
immigration--History--19th century--Juvenile literature. 3.
Emigration and immigration--History--Sources--Juvenile literature.
I. Title.

JV6351.H93 2015   j304.8'7   C2014-908083-2
                                           C2014-908084-0

Library of Congress Cataloging-in-Publication Data

Flatt, Lizann.
 Immigration / Lizann Flatt.
     pages cm. -- (Uncovering the past : analyzing primary
sources)
 Includes an index.
 ISBN 978-0-7787-1550-4 (reinforced library binding : alk.
paper) -- ISBN 978-0-7787-1554-2 (pbk. : alk. paper) -- ISBN
978-1-4271-1602-4 (electronic pdf) -- ISBN 978-1-4271-1598-0
(electronic html)
1. Emigration and immigration--Juvenile literature. 2.
Emigration and immigration--Research--Methodology--
Juvenile literatrue. I. Title.

 JV6201.F53 2015
 304.8--dc23
                                           2014047277

Crabtree Publishing Company

www.crabtreebooks.com   1-800-387-7650

Printed in Canada/022015/MA20150101

Published in Canada
Crabtree Publishing
616 Welland Ave.
St. Catharines, ON
L2M 5V6

Published in the United States
Crabtree Publishing
PMB 59051
350 Fifth Avenue, 59th Floor
New York, NY 10118

Published in the United Kingdom
Crabtree Publishing
Maritime House
Basin Road North, Hove
BN41 1WR

Published in Australia
Crabtree Publishing
3 Charles Street
Coburg North
VIC, 3058

UNCOVERING THE PAST
ANALYZING PRIMARY SOURCES

WHY LEARN ABOUT THE PAST?

"Give me your tired, your poor,
Your huddled masses yearning to breathe free,
The wretched refuse of your teeming shore.
Send these, the homeless, tempest-tost to me,
I lift my lamp beside the golden door!"

From "The New Colossus" by Emma Lazarus, written November 2, 1883, engraved on the pedestal of the Statue of Liberty in New York

Have you ever moved from one house or town to another? Maybe you or someone you know has moved from a different country to make a home here. When people leave one country to make a life in another, we call that **immigration**. The people who arrive in a new country are called **immigrants**.

People have always moved from place to place. They move to escape poverty or war. They search for a better life. They seek adventure and a fresh start, or freedom to practice their religion. From the first peoples who arrived in North America and the first European settlers up to the people who arrive here today, immigration has shaped the **history** of the countries on this continent from the very beginning.

When we talk about the past, we mean a time and events that have already happened. Why should we bother to learn about the past? The past is important because it has shaped the way things are today. Look around your neighborhood. Maybe the roads were first built by settlers. Perhaps nearby places are named by, or for, one of the first people to live there. Maybe you have festivals, or perhaps a food your region is famous for? They likely came about because of the early immigrants to your area.

▼ The Statue of Liberty was the first landmark that early immigrants saw when they arrived in the United States. It was a welcome symbol to immigrants. Almost 14 million immigrants arrived by ship at New York Harbor between 1886 and 1924.

DEFINITIONS

Immigration or **Emigration:** Which word should you use? Immigration is used to talk about people arriving in a country to settle down permanently. Emigration is used to talk about people permanently leaving a country. Similarly, immigrants are people who arrive to live in a new land. **Emigrants** are people who leave their country.

HOW DO WE FIND OUT ABOUT HISTORY?

History is the study of things that happened in the past. If no one is around to tell us what happened long ago, how do we know what took place? Luckily, the people who lived in the past left behind clues to what their lives were like. When we discover these clues today, we investigate and examine them to form reasonable conclusions about their lives.

What sorts of things did people leave behind? People built homes and villages, and roads or paths. They threw away things they no longer had a use for. When people died, they were buried. All these things can be discovered by **historians** today.

Historians are people who study history. They look at these discoveries and make educated guesses about what the past was like. This makes historians a little like detectives. Many things, such as remains of buildings, roads, and such household items as pots or furniture, are unearthed or discovered, then studied.

DEFINITIONS

Historians have special words to talk about time. Here is what they mean:

Decade: 10 years
Century: 100 years
Millennium: 1,000 years
Generation: A description of a time period when a group of people were born, such as the Baby Boomer Generation. Parents are a separate generation from their children.
Era: A description of a time period dominated by an important event, characteristic, or person, for example, the Steam Era or the Civil Rights Era.
Age: A description of a long period of time that is dominated by an important event, person, or characteristic, such as the Ice Age.

▶ Places that were historically important are often turned into museums or historic sites. Interpreters, such as these women dressed as nurses at Grosse Île, and the Irish Memorial National Historic Site in Canada, help visitors to learn what life was like in the past.

"Think—how different life is here in America, my Loris, you will realize that when you come, they live in comfort and abundance, nothing is missing, there is even too much and the cakes are more than enough."

Letter from Antonietta Petris, Montreal, September 26, 1948

Sometimes historians learn about the past because people have saved things. Some objects that people value are passed down from generation to generation, such as pieces of art, family photographs, jewelry, and **heirloom** antiques.

People also pass stories down from generation to generation. These oral histories preserve history.

Newspapers record the news and opinions of the time in which they were published. Writers and artists recorded their impressions of what they saw around them. Some people wrote about how they wanted to stop certain types of people from coming to North America. Others wanted to let everyone have a chance at a new life. Just as the newspapers, magazines, and other **media** today report different and often contradictory opinions on current events, not everyone had the same opinion or saw things the same way in the past either. Historians have to be careful to look at lots of different **evidence**.

▲ Illustrations in magazines or newspapers record what happened or what some people's opinions were at that time.

TYPES OF EVIDENCE

"Free / Only want to be free
We huddle close / Hang on to a dream
On the boats and on the planes
They're coming to America
Never looking back again
They're coming to America"

Song lyrics to "America" by Neil Diamond, 1980

A historical source is anything that tells us about the past. It can be a physical object, an image, something written down, or something you listen to. But no matter what the source is, there are two main types of historical information: **primary sources** and **secondary sources**.

A primary source gives firsthand knowledge of a topic. It was created by someone who participated in or witnessed the topic or event. Primary sources can be kept in museums, libraries, or private collections. Primary sources are:

Created when an event happened, or very soon afterward

Created by someone who saw, heard, or experienced the event

It can take a researcher a long time to track down enough primary sources to come up with evidence to form a reliable conclusion about a historic event or time period. Historians take years to analyze primary sources.

▶ The journey from Europe to North America by sailing ship took up to two months. By the time steamships were common, the trip took no more than ten days. No matter how long it took, the crossing would be one that many immigrants recorded in stories and letters.

SECONDARY SOURCES

Historians publish articles or papers on their findings. An artist consults primary sources to create a painting of a historic event. A writer interviews people and writes about events these people once experienced. These articles, paintings, and books are secondary sources.

Secondary sources are created after an event happened by someone who finds, interprets, or collects primary evidence. They can be very accurate sources of information if the person who created them was very careful and thorough with their research. Secondary sources are much easier to find than primary sources, but they won't all agree about past events. Different historians can come to different conclusions. **Bias**—the writer's opinions—can come into secondary evidence. Sometimes what you think of something depends on your point of view, and that can change how you interpret things.

CREATING A RECORD

Have you ever kept a journal to remember a trip? Or sent an email or updated your social media to tell a friend about where you went and what you saw? You'd probably write down how you felt about those things, perhaps expressing boredom or fascination. Letters like these have been preserved and tell us much about life in the past.

Immigration from one country to another also creates paperwork. To leave their country, immigrants had to buy a ticket on a ship. Ships had to keep lists of their passengers for each voyage. Immigrants carried immigration papers, such as birth certificates, marriage licenses, or passports, to prove who they were and where they came from.

"There was nothing but land; not a country at all, but the material out of which countries are made."

Willa Cather, *My Ántonia*, the story of an immigrant girl in Nebraska, published 1918

▲ The same way you have to buy a bus or plane ticket to take a trip, immigrants purchased tickets to board ships to take them to North America. This 1913 ticket is a piece of primary evidence.

TYPES OF SOURCES

Primary written sources include:

- The diary or journal of someone who experienced the topic or event you're researching
- Interviews with people who experienced the event
- Newspaper articles about current events or topics
- Census data
- Documents and letters created at the time
- Passports, birth certificates, and other official papers
- Tickets for ship travel
- Ships' lists of passengers
- Emails
- Poems and song lyrics

Secondary written sources include:

- Encyclopedias
- Textbooks
- Newspaper or magazine articles about an event in the past
- Poems and song lyrics

Laws are made to govern a country. When a country makes a law, it is dated and written down so that the meaning of the law is clear. Laws were enacted over the years to say who would and would not be allowed into the country. Governments also keep information about their **citizens**. They take a regular count of how many adults there are, where they live, where they were born, how many children they have, and other information. This gathering of information is called a **census**. All these documents create primary sources to study.

▼ Immigrants who bought the least expensive tickets were called steerage passengers. They often had to sleep on deck out in the open.

11

DIFFERENT SOURCES

Have you ever snapped a photograph to remember an event? Maybe you've drawn a picture or a diagram to remember something. Visual sources can be important pieces of evidence for historians. Immigrants had pictures taken of their new homes. Artists painted some of their experiences. Newspapers included sketches and, later, photographs to help people understand the news they were reading.

Places can also be important sources of information about the past. Immigrants who arrived at ports had to be examined and questioned at immigration stations. These stations include Ellis Island and Angel Island in

ANALYZE THIS

Is a modern photograph of a historic site primary evidence or secondary evidence? When you make a social media status update, are you creating primary evidence or secondary evidence?

◄ Ellis Island, New York, was an immigration station that was the entry point to the U.S. for 12 million immigrants from 1892 to 1954. The site is now preserved as a museum, and helps us understand what it was like to arrive as an immigrant in the past.

"Canada, the blest—the free!
With prophetic glance, I see
Visions of thy future glory,
Giving to the world's great story
A page, with mighty meaning fraught,
That asks a wider range of thought."

Susanna Moodie, *Roughing it in the Bush*, an autobiographical story of a British immigrant settling in Canada in 1852

DIFFERENT SOURCES

Primary visual, audio, or physical sources include:
  Photographs taken at the time of the event or place
  Maps from the time period you're researching
  Diagrams drawn at the time you're researching
  Artifacts

Recorded interviews of people who experienced the event

Secondary visual, audio or physical sources include:
  Maps created today to show historical information

Interviews with an expert on a topic unless the person directly experienced the topic or event
Photographs of a historic site
Reproductions of items used in the past

the United States, and Grosse Île and Pier 21 in Canada. Each of these places has been turned into a museum or state park, where visitors can learn more about immigration in the past.

When you go to a big event, such as a concert or sports game, do you ever buy a souvenir? Or perhaps you've saved a prize-winning ribbon or a trophy? People save things that have meaning for them. Even though people throw things away, they are preserved in dumps.

Has someone older than you ever taught you a song that they learned when they were young? Songs are passed down through generations. The words record how people felt or the experiences people had. Recorded songs provide future generations with clues about what concerned people at that time.

◄ This medical wagon is on display at Grosse Île museum in Canada. It can tell us how immigrants needing medical care were moved from the ships to the hospital.

INTERPRETATION

"I do not care what language a man speaks, or what religion he professes, if he is honest and law-abiding, if he will go on that land and make a living for himself and his family, he is a desirable settler for the Dominion of Canada . . ."

Clifford Sifton, statement to the Canadian House of Commons while Minister of the Interior, July 1899

Photographs provide good evidence about what life was like in the past. But photographs need to be analyzed. Historians look carefully at the images and ask questions. To get information from an old photograph, you need to take time to look at it carefully. Try this with the photograph on the right.

Look at the people first. How are they dressed? Are they wealthy? Was the photograph taken for a special occasion? How old are the people? Can you see their facial expressions? How do you think they feel?

Look at objects in the photograph. Are people holding things? If you don't know what some of the objects are, ask your teacher or a librarian. Find out how the items were used.

Look carefully at the background. Does it tell you where the photograph was taken? Can you tell what time of year it is?

Historians look at other primary sources to **verify** their conclusions. Do images ever lie? To answer that question, have you ever altered a photograph so that it looks different? Photographs are good sources of information, but they must be analyzed for accuracy.

▶ Immigrants lined up as they waited to be examined and questioned at immigration stations. After their long voyage across the ocean, they were about to find out if they would be allowed into their new country.

ANALYZE THIS

Before the technology for color photographs was possible, black-and-white photographs were hand colored. A person called a colorist applied a light layer of oil paint over the black-and-white photograph. Do you think the colors are accurate? Is there a chance that bias could come in?

EVIDENCE RECORD CARD

Immigrants at Ellis Island
LEVEL Primary source
MATERIAL Oil paint over photograph
  Photographer: Unknown
LOCATION Ellis Island, New York
DATE About 1900
SOURCE The Granger Collection

HOW HISTORIANS INTERPRET EVIDENCE

Historians are like detectives. They take clues from primary sources and form conclusions based on studying them. They go through a process that asks questions such as these:

What is the source?

Why was this source created?

When was this source created?

What else was going on at about the same time?

What does the source prove, claim, show, or say?

Do other primary sources say the same or different things?

As new sources are discovered, new information comes to light about events that happened in the past. Historians try to be responsible and interpret things as accurately as possible so that untruths do not get spread around as truth. Historians do not always agree because they can come to very different conclusions about the same piece of evidence. Or perhaps there is important information they haven't yet discovered, or even evidence that is permanently

▲ **Immigrants often worked at home doing piecework.** This meant they were paid by the number of pieces they could complete. These immigrants are carrying home garments to sew.

HOW TO RECORD EVIDENCE

When historians make conclusions, they cite, or state, the sources of information they studied. They give as much information about these sources as possible, so that others can also track down these sources to do their own research. This information, called a **citation**, which is usually gathered in a **bibliography** of a written work, includes what the evidence is, where it was found, when it was created, who created it, and where it was created.

lost. This can mean they come to incorrect conclusions.

It's hard to look at evidence and stay totally **objective**. Sometimes, our own thoughts and beliefs cloud our opinions of the things we see or read. Artists in favor of immigration might paint pictures of immigrant families joyfully arriving in a new land. Those who oppose immigration could paint immigrants as ugly, dirty, or as people their homeland is happy to get rid of. Similarly, if a company or government wanted to attract immigrants, they would write about the many immigrants who now make money by working their own farmland. Someone who is against immigration might choose to focus on those immigrants who are barely making enough money to eat while struggling with the backbreaking work of farming.

PERSPECTIVES

The messages an image shows can depend on the beliefs and experiences of the viewer. Do you think the illustration opposite shows hardworking and ambitious immigrants eager to get to work? Or do you think it shows these immigrants to be burdened by the weight of all the work they have to do to survive?

▼ This cartoon from 1880 shows Uncle Sam, representing the United States, welcoming all types of immigrants under the cloud of war. The original caption proclaimed "Welcome to All!"

IMMIGRATION

"We came to America, either ourselves or in the persons of our ancestors, to better the ideals of men, to make them see finer things than they had seen before, to get rid of the things that divide and to make sure of the things that unite."

President Woodrow Wilson addressing naturalized citizens at Convention Hall, Philadelphia, May 10, 1915

No one knows exactly who first settled in North America. Aboriginal, or first, people are believed to have traveled from Asia across a land bridge between Siberia and Alaska. Historians think there were about 350,000 Aboriginal people in Canada in about the year 1000 C.E. In America, there were about 900,000 Native peoples when the first European settlers arrived in the 1500s.

Long poems passed down from generation to generation told of Viking **settlements** in North America. Leif Eriksson was the first European to arrive in North America in about 1000 C.E. Remains of a Viking settlement were discovered at L'Anse aux Meadows in today's Newfoundland. About 100 Vikings settled there and built **sod-walled** homes.

The European explorers, beginning with Columbus in 1492, felt they had discovered a new world. Spain and Portugal set up the first **colonies**. France, Holland, and Britain soon followed. In 1564, Huguenots, or French **Protestants**, escaped persecution in France and started a colony near Jacksonville, Florida. In 1608, Samuel de Champlain started a settlement where Quebec City, Canada, is today.

▶ The first European immigrants settled together in locations called colonies. Within a few centuries, European immigrants built cities and changed the whole makeup of society in North America.

ANALYZE THIS

Look carefully at what the people in this photograph are doing. Are there things you see here that you'd see in a city today? What things are different from today?

THE FIRST COLONIES

The British established their first settlement at Jamestown on Chesapeake Bay in 1607. In 1624, the first Dutch settlers arrived in what they called New Amsterdam. This grew into today's New York City. Thousands of colonists settled in North America, part of **The New World**. Many of the settlements survived with help from Native peoples. In the 1700s, **Amish**, **Quakers**, and **Mennonites** left Germany for religious freedom in America. By 1790, as many as 100,000 Germans had emigrated to America.

Irish immigrants first arrived in large numbers in the 1720s. Beginning in about 1780, many Scottish **tenant** farmers were forced off the hills in Scotland by landowners who wanted to turn from farming to more profitable sheep herding. These Scottish Highlanders settled in present-day Nova Scotia, Prince Edward Island, Ontario, and Manitoba in Canada, and in Charleston and Jamestown in the United States.

The increase of so many Europeans through the 1700s brought more contact with European diseases to the Native

▶ African-American slaves were forced to work and live on the **plantations** and farms in the New World. These are old slavery cabins at a former plantation in South Carolina. It is estimated that by 1830 there were more than 2 million slaves living in the United States.

"A great blessing meets the German emigrant the moment he steps upon these shores: he comes into a free country; free from the oppression of despotism . . . free from the pressure of intolerable taxes . . . free from constraint in matters of belief and conscience."

F. W. Bogen, *The German in America: Or, Advice and instruction for German emigrants in the United States of America*, published in German in 1851

Americans. They also faced competition for the use of land. Many tribes were confined to **reservations**. These and other factors caused a drop in the Native population and the destruction of their traditional way of life.

SLAVERY

Unlike other immigrant groups, West Africans were forced to come to North America. The Spanish, Portuguese, Dutch, French, and British all captured West Africans from their villages and brought them to North America as slaves. The slaves were bought and sold, and forced to work the plantations and farms in the Americas. Between 15 and 20 million Africans were taken in the 300 years of slavery. Not all black people in the United States were slaves. There were also freed slaves and their children, escaped slaves, and those who lived where slavery was abolished. By 1790, there were about 60,000 free African Americans living in the United States. By 1830, the number rose to about 300,000.

ANALYZE THIS

With the increase in the number of people coming to North America, what impact do you think was felt by the population and way of life of the Native American tribes?

▶ After the American Revolution of 1775–1783, people of German, black, Native, or British background who wanted to stay loyal to Great Britain moved to Canada because it was still ruled by the British.

THE NINETEENTH CENTURY

The 1800s brought a huge increase in immigration to North America by many different European nationalities. The United States expanded its land from the Atlantic to the Pacific coasts. The country was seen as a land of plenty, and a land of freedom from the economic hardships and religious traditions of Europe.

Between 1774 and 1844, nearly 1 million Irish people immigrated to the United States. Many were **artisans** or skilled workers, so they quickly found success in their new life. Unskilled immigrants went to work on huge projects such as the construction of the Erie Canal or the railroads.

In 1845, a fungus attacked the potato crop in Ireland and ruined this important food source. The population of Ireland dropped from about 8 million before the famine to 5 million afterward. About 1 million died from hunger or disease. Many emigrated to North America. They were packed on ships that were so crowded and **unsanitary,** they were called coffin ships. They arrived penniless at New York and Grosse Île. These newer **Roman Catholic** immigrants settled with people of their own background in cities, creating the first **ethnic** neighborhoods in North America.

Nearly 1 million Germans immigrated to the United States in the 1850s and

◄ Hundreds of thousands of Irish peasants were evicted from their cottages when the potato famine meant they couldn't pay their rent. Some landowners paid to send their former tenants overseas, as it was cheaper than paying taxes to raise funds to help them.

▲ Chinese immigrants first came to North America looking for "The Gold Mountain" during the gold rush. Most were disappointed but could not afford the trip back home.

settled to farm the valleys of the Mississippi, Missouri, and Ohio rivers. Others moved to the cities to work as skilled tradespeople or found work in new factories in the city centers.

When gold was discovered in California in 1848, immigrants from all over the world came to mine for gold. American tradespeople and entrepreneurs headed west to make a living off the miners. The largest group of immigrants joining in the **gold rush** were young men from China. By 1851, about 25,000 had arrived. More gold was soon discovered in British Columbia and Yukon. Americans or Chinese who had failed to find gold in California tried their luck farther north.

ANALYZE THIS

Look carefully at the photograph of the Chinese family. It is a black-and-white photograph that has been colorized by hand. Do you think the facial color the colorist used reflects reality? How might bias come in?

"Saturday, April 27. Cooked our breakfast with peagrass and ready for a start by six o'clock . . . At eight o'clock we passed eight or ten graves of last year's emigrants. At twelve we stopped for dinner . . . At six o'clock we encamped for the night on the bank of a creek, with plenty of wood and water, but grass scarce. Traveled this day fifteen miles."

James Abbey, "California: A Trip Across the Plains," 1850

The development of iron steamships after 1855 meant that voyages from Europe could take as little as ten days. Fares became cheaper and the steamships were bigger and more comfortable. New railroads were also built. These needed laborers, notably the Chinese on the Central Pacific Railroad and the Irish on the Union Pacific Railroad. These two railroads joined tracks on May 10, 1869, in Utah to form the first American transcontinental railroad. Immigrants who arrived at Ellis Island could now take the train far inland or even all the way to the Pacific Coast to start their new lives.

▼ Railways looked to expand as quickly and cheaply as possible. Camps with workers' families were set up along the line.

"Ma the longer I stay here the better I like it, there are but very few old families here they are mostly young families just starting in life the same as we are and I find them very generous indeed. We will all be poor here together and grow up together and I hope be happy together."

Letter from Uriah W. Oblinger, December 1, 1872

In Canada, 15,000 Chinese laborers worked on railroad construction, especially the Canadian Pacific Railway through British Columbia that was completed by 1885. Many of those that survived the dangers stayed in Canada, as they could not afford the fare home.

NEW FARMS

In 1862, the United States passed the Homestead Act. This gave free land to people who would work it into farmland for a minimum of five years. A shortage of farmland, then famine in Sweden in the late 1860s, caused about 1 million Swedes to immigrate to the United States from 1868 to 1914. Many settled on the prairies. Between 1825 and 1925, about 800,000 Norwegians settled in Minnesota, Iowa, Wisconsin, and North Dakota. Danish immigrants who had converted to the **Mormon** religion settled in Utah, while others settled in Michigan, Wisconsin, Illinois, and the Dakotas. About 300,000 Danish people immigrated from 1820 to 1920. From 1890 to 1924, about 230,000 Finnish people arrived to settle near the Great Lakes to farm or to work in lumber mills. The heaviest period of German immigration occurred in the 1880s, as 1.5 million Germans arrived to settle in Texas and the Dakotas.

This heavy wave of immigration caused an anti-immigration backlash. An economic depression in the 1870s created competition for jobs. The Chinese Exclusion Act of 1882 prevented Chinese from immigrating to America on penalty of imprisonment or deportation.

▼ The dangerous trip overland to California by Conestoga wagon could take as long as six months. Before the transcontinental railway was completed, it was the most popular way to travel.

INDEPENDENT CANADA

In 1867, Canada became an independent **dominion** within the British Empire. The United States had a transcontinental railroad, so Canada needed one, too. Once it was completed in 1885, Canada could settle its western territories.

Most European immigrants had chosen the United States. Some immigrants came to Canada for a time, then moved to the United States. But several groups of immigrants did settle in the new province of Manitoba and other parts of the West. Mennonites and Jews from Russia fled from religious persecution. Scandinavian immigrants established communities on the prairies. Polish immigrants settled on farmland in

▼ A view inside a sleeping car on the Canadian Pacific Railway, 1888.

"I could not believe it possible that here, within reach of help, we should be left as neglected as when upon the ocean. That after a voyage of two months' duration we were to be left still enveloped by reeking pestilence, the sick without medicine, medical skill, nourishment or so much as a drop of pure water . . ."

Irish emigrant Robert Whyte on his voyage to Quebec, Canada, July 28, 1848 eastern Ontario and in the West, especially around Winnipeg.

Many single women immigrated to Canada as domestic servants, especially from Britain. Beginning in about 1870, agencies started to sponsor children aged 6 to 15 to come to Canada. These were orphaned children sent to work on farms or as domestic servants. About 40,000 of these Home Children came to Canada between 1870 and 1897. Many were badly treated and worked long hours, or were physically or emotionally abused.

A NEW START

In 1896, Canadian immigration policy changed dramatically. Canada wanted to settle the West to prevent the United States from taking the land. Clifford Sifton was the **minister** responsible for immigration. He increased advertising in Britain, Europe, and the United States, promising prosperity in Canada for all. He hired agents to persuade American and British farmers to immigrate to Canada with the promise of up to 160 acres of free land, although settlers had to pay $10 as a land registration fee.

Sifton's slogan was "Canada: The Last Best West." More than 3 million people came to Canada between 1896 and 1914. Of these, about 1 million were Americans. While many settled on farms in the West or moved to remote areas to work in the lumber or mining industries or on the new railroads, about half settled in the major cities such as Montreal, Toronto, Calgary, Winnipeg, and Edmonton.

▼ This farmstead in Canada was home to new immigrants in about 1890.

THE NEW CENTURY

Beginning in about 1900, the population of the United States began to move to the cities looking for wealth. Increasing numbers of factories provided work for many unskilled laborers. During this period, immigrants came mainly from non-English speaking countries, especially Italy, Poland, and Russia.

Italian immigration to the United States began slowly. Skilled craftspeople, musicians, artists, and shopkeepers made their homes in many different parts of the country. Between 1820 and 1870, fewer than 25,000 Italian immigrants arrived. By 1920, however, more than 4 million Italians had arrived. They came because of political conflict, natural disasters, and famine in Italy. Most of these immigrants were farm workers and laborers looking for work. A large number were single men.

Many sent a large part of their earnings back home to Italy. Some men worked for a while in the United States, then returned home. Many of these immigrants remained in New York City, where they had arrived through Ellis Island. They settled in neighborhoods with Italians they knew from home. Many had to take low-paying factory jobs in unsafe working conditions. Others moved across the country, working in farms, shipyards, mines, or quarries.

ANALYZE THIS

Look at the advertisement and study the wording. Which parts of the advertisement are designed to catch your attention? Which parts contain practical information? Could this poster convince someone to immigrate?

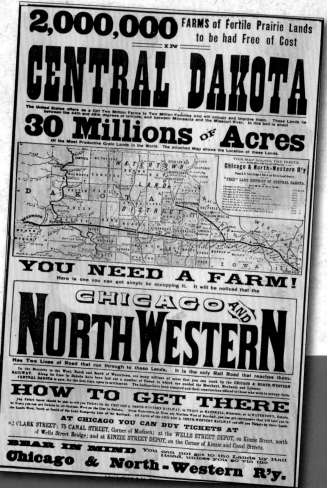

▶ Advertisements for free farmland enticed Europeans to immigrate to North America.

FROM FAR AND WIDE

Jews from Eastern Europe, especially Russia, fled religious persecution and economic hardship to seek freedom and prosperity. About 200,000 Jews arrived in the 1880s, and more than 300,000 in the 1890s. From 1900 to 1914, the number rose to about 1.4 million. Most of these Jews settled in New York City, especially on the Lower East Side.

Japanese immigrants arrived in the United States between 1886 and 1911. Japan's **urbanization** and **industrialization** left many farmers without land. In the 1880s, Japan began to allow selected citizens to emigrate. About 400,000 immigrated to America during that time. When they arrived, they settled in Hawaii, where many worked on plantations, or along the Pacific Coast, where many became farm workers or worked in mines or canneries, or on railroads. Many went on to prosper and own their own businesses or land.

▼ This photograph from 1942 shows a Japanese American family. The father and mother (center) immigrated to the United States from Japan, and their 11 children were born in the United States.

WAR AND PEACE

During the 1920s, about a million Canadians left for the United States, seeking better jobs. Canada then faced labor shortages in mining, pulp and paper, and other manufacturing industries. The government continued to favor white Americans, British, and northern Europeans but, in 1926, opened up immigration to Central, Eastern, and Southern Europeans. Germans, Mennonites from America and Russia, Ukrainians, and Polish immigrants were among those who arrived.

The U.S. economy boomed in the 1920s. Unemployment and land shortages in Poland meant that as many as 2 million Polish immigrants arrived by the late 1920s. Many settled in the farming regions of Wisconsin, Michigan, and Minnesota. Others settled in the industrial cities of Pittsburg, Cleveland, Detroit, Milwaukee, Buffalo, Chicago, and New York.

The Stock Market Crash of 1929, and the economic disaster of the Great Depression of the 1930s, caused a worldwide economic disaster. The Canadian government stopped almost all immigration. Drought added to the problems in North America. It is estimated that 400,000 people left the Great Plains region.

The impact of World War II was immense. After it finished in

◀ This poster from 1917 has a message in Hebrew to new Jewish immigrants to the United States, urging them not to waste the wheat that was needed to feed the Allied armies during World War I.

1945, many Europeans had no homes and became **displaced persons**. From 1945 to 1955, more than a million of them came to Canada. Most had no money, identification papers, or family to help them get started in their new country.

Many soldiers had married while fighting in Europe. Canadian soldiers brought their war brides and new children back to Canada. Nearly 50,000 women and 22,000 children had arrived by the end of 1946. Similarly, the United States enacted the War Brides Act in 1945, admitting 115,000 British, 7,000 Chinese, 5,000 Filipino, and 800 Japanese wives, and 25,000 children, as well as 20,000 **fiancées**.

After World War II, the Canadian government wanted immigrants because it needed workers. Many immigrants wanted to come to Canada because it was a safe place to live. Overall, about 2.5 million people arrived between 1946 and 1965. Both Canada and the United States moved toward more inclusive laws to accept people from across the world.

▶ After World War II, **refugees** and displaced persons arrived by ship to start new lives in the United States and Canada. Many of these new immigrants already had families and friends in the two countries.

PERSPECTIVES

During wartime, many people of German, Chinese, Japanese, Italian, Ukrainian, Jewish, and other backgrounds faced prejudice in the United States and Canada, even if they'd been born in North America. Some citizens were even put in jail or forced to leave their homes and businesses to live in **internment camps** for the rest of the war.

NEW CHALLENGES

"Remember, remember always that all of us, and you and I especially, are descended from immigrants and revolutionists."

President Franklin D. Roosevelt addressing the Daughters of the American Revolution, April 21, 1938

To know who was entering the country, and from where, governments established places where they could record immigrants and exclude certain types of people from getting in. Governments didn't want to look after people unable to find work. They also wanted to protect their citizens from **contagious** diseases. **Quarantine** stations were set up to secure immigrants who might be ill, so they could recover before being allowed into the country.

Before 1890, immigration to the United States was handled by individual states. The federal government then took over this role. On January 1, 1892, the first federal immigration station opened at Ellis Island in New York. At that time, the only way to get to North America was by ship. Most immigrants entered the United States through New York because it was the most popular steamship port. Passengers had to pass a medical inspection. On the West Coast, Angel Island opened in 1910 and performed a similar job. The majority of immigrants arriving here were Asian.

In Canada, Grosse Île at the port of Quebec was the first immigration station, operating from 1832 to 1937. Later, Pier 21 in Halifax, Nova Scotia, became the main Canadian immigration port. A medical exam and an interview by an immigration officer were required before being admitted to Canada.

▶ During its heaviest use between 1900 and 1914, more than 5,000 people could pass through the Ellis Island immigration processing station every day.

ASIAN ENTRY

Countries make laws to keep out people they don't want in the country, such as sick people or criminals. But sometimes they make laws to prevent people from specific countries from immigrating. Both the U.S. and Canadian governments targeted the Chinese, as their culture was distinctly different from that of other immigrant groups.

The Chinese Exclusion Act of 1882 was the first law to restrict immigration into the United States. For the next ten years, Chinese men couldn't enter the country or they'd be imprisoned or **deported** back to China. It made the Chinese who were already in the country permanent **aliens**: They could not become citizens. In 1892, the law was renewed, then made permanent in 1902. During the 1920s, new laws tightened restrictions on immigration before the 1929 National Origins Act limited all immigration to the United States to 150,000 persons and prohibited Asian immigration altogether. This was repealed in 1943, when the Magnuson Act allowed 105 Chinese into the United States each year. The Immigration and Nationality Act of 1965 got rid of all regulations about where immigrants came from and finally allowed large numbers of Chinese to immigrate to the United States.

In Canada, similar anti-Chinese policies were put into effect. In 1885, a $10 fee was charged to every Chinese immigrant entering the country, a fee that reached $500 in 1903. The Chinese

▶ Part of the U.S. Immigration Act of 1917 required that people aged more than 16 be able to read in any language. Immigrants were given 30 to 40 words to read aloud to prove they could read. This test is printed with Armenian script at the top and English at the bottom.

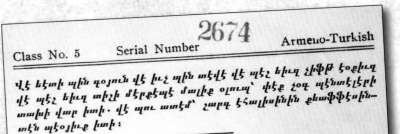

Class No. 5 Serial Number 2674 Armeno-Turkish

His substance also was seven thousand sheep, and three thousand camels, and five hundred yoke of oxen, and five hundred she asses, and a very great household; so that this man was the greatest of all the men of the east.

(Job 1:3)

"Our best interests are suffering of these Asiatic slaves; we are trying to make them live decently while here, and to discourage their arrival in such numbers as to drive white laborers out of the country."

San Francisco real estate flyer, September 1874

Immigration Act of 1923 restricted almost all immigration from China. Between 1923 and 1946, only about 15 Chinese people immigrated to Canada. Immigration regulations in 1962 finally got rid of racially based criteria. An immigrant's skill became the main criteria for being allowed into the country.

Both Canada and the United States also restricted immigration from Japan. In 1908, the two governments both reached agreement with the Japanese government. The United States agreed to allow only family members of current Japanese residents to enter the country, while the Canadian government limited the number of Japanese entering Canada to 400 persons a year. The Continuous Journey Regulation of 1908 said that only immigrants who arrived in Canada with direct tickets from their country of origin could be allowed into Canada. This cut off most Japanese immigration, as the route from Japan was often by way of Hawaii.

▶ *Puck* was a **satirical** magazine published from 1877 to 1918. The cover of this issue shows **anarchists**, Russians, Jews, and Italians dressed in kimonos, the traditional clothing of Japan, being kept out of the United States.

▼ New immigrants could often only afford to live with other families together in crowded housing called **tenements**. Sometimes, a family only had one room to live in.

ETHNIC NEIGHBORHOODS

Immigrants often settle in neighborhoods with people of the same background. This creates ethnic neighborhoods or **enclaves**. An ethnic neighborhood has signs in a language that is not English, and businesses, such as restaurants and grocery stores, that sell foods specific to a different country. Other products and services are offered to people in their native language. Some people feel ethnic neighborhoods help ease new immigrants into the new culture of North America. Others believe they just prolong or prevent new arrivals from **assimilating,** or blending into their new country.

Imagine coming to a country where you don't speak the language, and everything about it—from how people dress to how they eat—is unfamiliar to you. You would probably stay with a

▼ Ethnic neighborhoods where immigrants can find goods and services in their native language are found in cities and suburbs all over North America.

friend or someone who spoke your language if you could. In the same way, immigrants often move into areas where they find people with the same background. It helps them feel a little more familiar with their surroundings.

Another reason immigrants form ethnic neighborhoods is that it allows them to maintain their traditional way of life. They can find foods they are familiar with, and speak their native language. There may be places to practice their religion. New immigrants often need help getting started in their new country. Some may have little or no money, and no job. Established immigrants often help new immigrants with the same background. Sometimes, extended family members live together, sharing expenses, such as rent and food, and they help new arrivals to find a job.

Sometimes, it's not a matter of choice for immigrants to live in the same neighborhood. Often, new immigrants can only afford to live in the least expensive neighborhoods, so they go where they can afford to move in. Also, cities have been known to pass **bylaws** that restrict the types of people who live in certain areas. If many neighborhoods won't allow immigrants to live in them, then immigrants will live where they are able to.

ANALYZE THIS

What are some of the reasons that ethnic neighborhoods form?

◀ The film *West Side Story* from 1961 is the story of two New York City teens from different cultures who fall in love. Tony is American while Maria is a new immigrant from Puerto Rico. Their friends are rival gang members.

Skyscrapers bloom in America./Cadillacs zoom in America.

Industry boom in America./Twelve in a room in America.

Lots of new housing with more space./Lots of doors slamming in our face.

From "America," sung by Puerto Rican immigrants in *West Side Story*. Song lyrics by Stephen Sondheim, 1957.

RECENT IMMIGRATION

"Congressman, I have always argued that this country has benefited tremendously from the fact that we draw people from all over the world, and the average immigrant comes from a less [friendly] environment."

Federal Reserve Board Chairman Alan Greenspan
speaking to the U.S. Congress, July 18, 2001

Today people continue to immigrate to North America. Some are looking for the freedom and opportunities that are possible in the lifestyle that's available here. Others are forced to leave areas of war, poverty, or disaster to survive.

Both the United States and Canada wrestle with the challenges of welcoming people from other countries. A country has to look after its existing citizens, so it must decide what its rules will be for allowing new immigrants into the country. The economy and the amount of resources within the country are factors that governments need to evaluate. How many immigrants should be welcomed each year? Where do these immigrants come from? Are there enough jobs for everyone? Is there enough available housing for new immigrants? Can the country afford to give free education to more children? If people get sick, are there enough healthcare facilities to look after them? If people break the law, are there enough spaces in prison? These are some of the issues that governments must think about as they balance the needs of established citizens with immigrants wanting to become citizens.

▶ **Illegal immigrants** from Mexico are questioned at Border Control, having been caught and sent back from the United States. Some sources report that as many as 12 million illegal immigrants currently live in the country.

PERSPECTIVES

Look at the people in this photograph. Can you identify the Border Patrol officer? How can you tell which person it is? How do you think the men lining up might be feeling? What makes you think that?

ILLEGAL IMMIGRATION

One of the largest issues facing countries today is **undocumented immigrants**. An undocumented immigrant is someone living in a country without the government's permission to do so. They were not born in that country, so they are not citizens of the country they are living (and possibly working) in. They're also called aliens, **illegal aliens**, or illegal immigrants.

How do undocumented immigrants get inside the country in the first place? Some slip across the border without being caught. They might cross at nighttime in remote areas or get smuggled in. Others have received a **visa** to visit, stay, or work for a set period of time, but continued to stay in the country after the visa expired.

ANALYZE THIS

Look carefully at the airport photograph to the right. Now look at the small photograph on page 3 that shows a **reenactment** of immigration processing on Ellis Island. What things have changed? What is the same? Can you make a guess about what might be inaccurate about the reenactment?

▶ Airports are now the most popular way for people to arrive in a new country. Some come for a visit, while others hope to stay permanently. On a typical day in 2013, U.S. Customs and Border Protection looked over the documents of 280,059 international air passengers and crew.

"I believe that my parents, like so many other immigrants, dreamed their children into being as Canadians. . . . It is customary to talk about how hard immigrants work and how ambitious they are, but those of us who have lived that process, know that it is mainly the dream that counts."

Adrienne Clarkson, former Governor General of Canada, at her installation on October 7, 1999

Illegal immigrants are looking for a better way of life in the same way all other immigrants are. They want to work to earn money for themselves and their family. Some people feel that illegal immigrants take jobs away from citizens. Others feel that these immigrants perform necessary work in the economy by filling job vacancies that citizens don't want. Illegals will work for less money than citizens because any income is better than no income. Businesses benefit by paying less for the work they need done.

It is challenging for government officials to find undocumented immigrants. If they are found, they can be deported, or sent back to their country of birth. But what if these immigrants have children while here? Children become citizens of the country in which they are born. These children have the right to live in the United States or Canada, while their parents do not. Should the government separate the families by sending the parents back? Who would look after the child? Or should the government allow the parents to stay, work, and raise the child?

Countries also allow immigrants into the country because it is the compassionate thing to do. These are people whose homes, property, and way of life have been destroyed through natural disaster or war. They have nowhere to live and no way to make a living. These immigrants are called refugees because they are forced from their homes. But the same difficult questions about how to look after them, as well as existing citizens, are still widely debated today.

▼ In the late 1970s, about 1.5 million Vietnamese refugees fled their country in small, unsafe boats or fishing boats to escape war and a controlling government. Many died, but many began new lives in the United States, Canada, and other nations.

TIMELINE

1000 Vikings arrive in North America

1000

1400

1492 Christopher Columbus is the first European to reach North America

1500s French, Spanish, and Portuguese establish colonies in North America

1500

1600

1607 (U.S.) English establish Jamestown settlement in Virginia

1620 (U.S.) About 100 pilgrims arrive and establish a colony at Plymouth

1630s (U.S.) Puritans seek religious freedom and settle Massachusetts Bay colony

1700

1789 (U.S.) Constitution of the United States passed after the country becomes independent

1790 (U.S.) Naturalization Act gives citizenship to "free white persons" who have lived in the U.S. for 2 years

1800

1815 (U.S.) Immigrants from Western and Northern Europe begin to arrive in large numbers

1819 (U.S.) Congress passes act that requires ships to keep records of all immigrant passengers

1832 (C) Grosse Île quarantine station for Port of Quebec opens

1850

1848 (U.S.) Gold discovered in California, sparking a gold rush

1855 (U.S.) Castle Garden begins operation as New York port of entry

1862 (U.S.) Homestead Act gives up to 160 acres of free land in the West to settlers who will live on it for at least 5 years

1869 (U.S.) Transcontinental railroad completed

1875

1873 (C) Dominion Lands Act grants free 160-acre farms

1882 (U.S.) Chinese Exclusion Act passed

1882 (U.S.) Immigration Act puts 50-cent tax on every immigrant

1885 (C) Transcontinental railroad completed

1890s (U.S.) Immigration from Southern and Eastern Europe increases

1892 (U.S.) Opening of Ellis Island, the first U.S. federal immigration station

1896 (C) Gold discovered in the Klondike

1907 (U.S. & C) Gentlemen's agreements with Japan limit Japanese immigration

1910 (U.S.) Angel Island opens to process immigrants entering the U.S. on the Pacific Coast

1917 (U.S.) Immigration Act restricts immigration from Asia

1919 (C) Immigration Act limits undesirable immigrants based on nationality or race

1921 (C) Pier 21 opens in Halifax, Nova Scotia

1924 (U.S.) Immigration Act sets quotas on immigration

1900

2000

1929 (U.S.) National Origins Act sets maximum of 150,000 immigrants a year with no Asian immigration allowed

1952 (C) Immigration Act states preferred immigrants to be from Britain, France, and the U.S., plus Asians wanting to reunite with immediate family

1965 (U.S.) New maximum numbers of immigrants allowed on first-come first-served basis

1967 (C) Points system determines admission to Canada regardless of country of origin

Canada

Calgary

Vancouver

Seattle

Canada

Montreal

Minneapolis

Toronto · Boston

New York

Detroit · Philadelphia

Chicago · Washington

China
Japan
Other Asia

San Francisco

United States of America

Denmark
France
Germany
United Kingdom
Greece
Ireland
Italy
Norway
Sweden
Poland
Spain
Portugal
Russia
Other Europe

Los Angeles

Central and
Southern America
West Indies

N
W · E
S

Mexico

500 miles
500 km

BIBLIOGRAPHY

QUOTATIONS

p.6 Antonietta Petris quote:
https://umedia.lib.umn.edu/node/552681

p.10 Cather, Willa. *My Ántonia*. Houghton Mifflin, 1918.

p.12 Moodie, Susanna. *Roughing it in the Bush*. Richard Bentley, 1854.
www.gutenberg.org/files/4389/4389-h/4389-h.htm

p.14 Clifford Sifton quote:
www.historymuseum.ca/cmc/exhibitions/hist/advertis/ads4-03e.shtml

p.18 Woodrow Wilson quote:
www.presidency.ucsb.edu/ws/?pid=65388

p.20 Bogen, F.W. *The German in American, or Advice and Instruction for German Emigrants in the United States of America*. Trans. Boston, 1851.

p.23 Abbey, James. "California: A Trip Across the Plains." *California As I Saw It: First-Person Narratives, 1849–1900*. Library of Congress, 1997.
www.loc.gov/teachers/classroommaterials/presentationsandactivities/presentations/timeline/expref/oregtral/abbfour.html

p.24 Uriah W. Oblinger quote:
http://memory.loc.gov/cgi-bin/ampage?collId=nbhips&fileName=l084/nbhipsl084page.db&recNum=1&itemLink=r?ammem/psbib:@field%28DOCID+@lit%28l084%29%29

p.26 Conroy, Patrick. *Robert Whyte's 1847 Famine Ship Diary: The Journey of an Irish Coffin Ship*. Mercier Press, 1995.

p.32 Frankin D. Roosevelt quote:
www.presidency.ucsb.edu/ws/?pid=15631

p.34 Bayor, Ronald H. (Ed.) *The Columbia Documentary History of Race and Ethnicity in America*. Columbia University Press, 2004.

p.35 *Puck* magazine cover created by Frank A. Nankivell, Keppler & Schwarzmann, March 13, 1907.
www.loc.gov/pictures/item/2011647184/

p.37 "America" from the film *West Side Story*. Song lyrics by Stephen Sondheim, 1957.
www.youtube.com/watch?v=YhSKk-cvblc

p.38 Alan Greenspan quote:
www.gpo.gov/fdsys/pkg/CHRG-107hhrg74156/html/CHRG-107hhrg74156.htm

p.40 Adrienne Clarkson quote:
http://archive.gg.ca/media/doc.asp?lang=e&DocID=1379

BOOKS

Fine-Meyer, Rose. *The Immigrant Experience*. (Primary Documents of 20th Century Canada) Rubicon Publishing, 2003.

Hodge, Deborah. *The Kids Book of Canadian Immigration*. Kids Can Press, 2006.

Robbins, Albert. *Coming to America: Immigrants from Northern Europe*. Dell Publishing, 1982.

WEBSITES

Angel Island: Immigrant Journeys of Chinese Americans: www.angel-island.com/history.html

"Aspiration, Acculturation, and Impact: Immigration to the United States, 1789–1930": http://ocp.hul.harvard.edu/immigration/index.html

Caribou Gold Rush:
http://bcheritage.ca/cariboo/

Canadian Museum of Immigration at Pier 21:
www.pier21.ca/home/

Chinese in California, 1850–1925:
http://bancroft.berkeley.edu/collections/chineseinca/

Ellis Island: www.history.com/topics/ellis-island

Ellis Island: www.nps.gov/elis/index.htm

"Exploring the California Gold Rush" by Gary F. Kurutz: www.library.ca.gov/goldrush/

Immigration, Library of Congress:
www.loc.gov/teachers/classroommaterials/presentationsandactivities/presentations/immigration/index.html

Immigration History of Canada:
http://faculty.marianopolis.edu/c.belanger/quebechistory/encyclopedia/ImmigrationHistoryofCanada.htm

The Immigrant's Statue: www.nps.gov/stli/historyculture/the-immigrants-statue.htm

Irish Immigration to America 1846 to the early 20th century: www.irish-genealogy-toolkit.com/Irish-immigration-to-America.html

Klondike Gold Rush:
http://tc.gov.yk.ca/archives/klondike/en/prologue.html

Life and Death on Grosse Île, 1832–1937:
www.collectionscanada.gc.ca/grosse-ile/index-e.html

Moving Here, Staying Here: The Canadian Immigrant Experience:
www.collectionscanada.gc.ca/immigrants/index-e.html

INTERNET GUIDELINES

Finding good source material on the Internet can sometimes be a challenge. Analyze each site you find and check out the information on it. How reliable is it?

- Who writes and/or sponsors the page? Is it an expert in the field, a person who experienced the event, or just a person with an opinion?
- Is the site well known and up to date? Government and college websites often have lots of easy-to-find sources and information.
- Can you verify the facts with another source? Always double-check by comparing the information on several websites.
- Did you determine whether what you find is a primary source or secondary source? Do your secondary sources seem to be based on a variety of primary sources?
- Have you kept a list of the websites you've visited? This can help you verify information later.

TO FIND OUT MORE

Non-fiction:

Hearn, Emily, and Marywinn Milne (eds.). *Our New Home: Immigrant Children Speak*. Second Story Press, 2007.

Maestro, Betty. *Coming to America*. Scholastic Press, 1996.

Peacock, Louise. *At Ellis Island: A History in Many Voices*. Atheneum Books for Young Readers, 2007.

Fiction:

Fullerton, Alma. *Libertad*. Fitzhenry & Whiteside, 2008.

Paterson, Katherine. *The Day of the Pelican*. HMH Books for Young Readers, 2010.

Ryan, Pam Munoz. *Esperanza Rising*. Scholastic Press, 2002.

Tan, Shaun. *The Arrival*. Arthur A. Levine Books, 2007.

WEBSITES AND MULTIMEDIA

America on the Move: http://amhistory.si.edu/onthemove/exhibition/index.html

Canada Day 1: In their Own Words: www.pier21.ca/cd1/canada-day-1-oral-history-videos

Canadian Immigration Process: www.virtualmuseum.ca/Exhibitions/Pier 21/eng/etape1-step1-eng.html

Digitizing Immigrant Letters, Immigration History Research Centre, University of Minnesota: http://ihrc.umn.edu/research/dil/

Global Patterns of Human Migration: http://education.nationalgeographic.com/education/activity/global-patterns-human-migration/?ar_a=1

The Great American Potluck (Immigrants' recipes): www.loc.gov/teachers/classroommaterials/presentationsandactivities/presentations/immigration/ckbk/index.html

How the Other Half Lives: Studies among the Tenements of New York. Jacob A. Riis, New York: Charles Scribner's Sons, 1897: http://pds.lib.harvard.edu/pds/view/4137257?n=15&imagesize=1200&jp2Res=.5&printThumbnails=no

Interviews with Today's Immigrants: www.loc.gov/teachers/classroommaterials/presentationsandactivities/presentations/immigration/interv/toc.php

The Last Best West, Advertising for Immigrants to Western Canada, 1870–1930. Canadian Museum of History: www.historymuseum.ca/cmc/exhibitions/hist/advertis/adindexe.shtml

Oral Histories, Ellis Island. www.nps.gov/elis/historyculture/oral-histories.htm

GLOSSARY

alien A person who is not a citizen of the country they are living in

Amish Originally a Swiss group of Christians, known for their simple dress

anarchist A person who wants no government or order

artisan A skilled worker

assimilating Fitting in

bias Not being completely fair or objective; favoring one thing over another

bibliography A list of books and other sources consulted when writing a book, essay, or report

bylaw A law that applies to a local area

census An official count that records numbers of people and details about them

citation A statement that is referred to in a book

citizen A person who has full rights to live in a country

colony A territory settled by immigrants from another country

contagious Easily spread

deported To send someone out of a country back to the country they came from

displaced person Someone who has been forced from their home by war or famine

dominion An independent country within an empire

emigrant Someone who leaves a country to live elsewhere

emigration The process of leaving a country permanently to live elsewhere

enclave A place that is different or ethnically distinct from the places surrounding it

era A description of a time period dominated by an important characteristic, event, or person

ethnic From a specific cultural background; a group with similar characteristics of religion, race, or culture

evidence Proof that something happened

fiancée Woman engaged to be married

generation A description of a time period when a group of people were born; parents are a separate generation from their children

gold rush The movement of a large group of people to an area to search for and mine gold

heirloom Personal property handed down through the generations

historian A person who writes about or studies history

history Past events

illegal aliens People who are not citizens of the country they're living in and who are there against the law

illegal immigrants People who are not citizens of the country they're living in and who came there against the law

immigrant A person who enters a country to live there permanently

immigration The process of entering a country to live

there permanently

industrialization The process of creating new industries that become major sources of employment and wealth

internment camp A place where people are kept against their will

laws Rules made by governments

media Different forms of communication, such as radio and television

Mennonite A member of a Christian group dedicated to peace

minister A government official

Mormon A member of The Church of Jesus Christ of Latter-day Saints

New World, the The continent of America, as newly discovered by Europeans

objective The ability to judge things fairly and impartially

piecework Work that is paid for by the numbers of items produced

plantation An area of land planted with crops, once worked by slaves

primary source A firsthand memory, account, document, or artifact from the past that serves as a historical record about what happened at a particular event or time

Protestant A member of a Christian church who does not recognize the authority of the Catholic church

Quaker A member of the Religious Society of Friends, dedicated to peace

quarantine A period of separation from other people to ensure disease is not spread

reenactment The acting out of a past event or scene

refugee A person who has been forced to flee his or her own country because of war or disaster

reservation An area of land set aside for Native Americans to live on

Roman Catholic A follower of the Christian religion where the pope is the head of the church

satirical Criticizing or poking fun at a belief, situation, person, custom, or attitude

secondary source A historian's or artist's interpretation of a primary source

settlement A place where immigrants have settled

sod-walled A wall made of cut slabs or chunks of grassy earth

steerage The cheapest ticket to board a ship

tenant Someone who pays rent to stay somewhere

tenement A room or rooms where people live inside a house or apartment where others live

undocumented immigrants Immigrants who do not have birth certificates or other documents to prove their citizenship

unsanitary Unclean and unhealthy

urbanization The process of creating new towns and cities at the expense of the countryside

verify To test the truth or accuracy of something

visa A permit to stay in a country

INDEX